PRESENTED TO

_____

WITH LOVE FROM

_____

ON

_____

ZONDERKIDZ

The Tiny Truths Illustrated Bible
Copyright © 2019 by Tiny Truths, Inc.
Illustrations © 2019 by Tiny Truths, Inc.

Requests for information should be addressed to:

Zonderkidz, 3900 Sparks Drive SE, Grand Rapids, Michigan 49546

Library of Congress Cataloging-in-Publication Data

Names: Rivard, Joanna, author.
Title: The tiny truths illustrated Bible / by Joanna Rivard and Tim Penner.
Description: Grand Rapids : Zonderkidz, 2019. |
Identifiers: LCCN 2018037446 (print) | LCCN 2018044434 (ebook) |
ISBN 9780310764335 | ISBN 9780310764311 (hardcover)
Subjects: LCSH: Bible stories, English.
Classification: LCC BS551.3 (ebook) | LCC BS551.3 .R578 2019 (print) | DDC 220.95/05—dc23
LC record available at https://lccn.loc.gov/2018037446

Art direction: Ron Huizinga
Illustrations: Tim Penner

Printed in China

22 23 /DSC/ 10 9 8 7 6 5 4

——————— FOR ———————

Grace, Oliver, Isaac, Jesse, and Clarabel
With so much love—Jo

———————————

Eli, Avery, Mahli, Mikayla, and Rylee
Five of my favorite people—Love Tim

———————————

With Special Thanks ...

for the creativity, insight, expertise, patience,
and love of our amazing families and friends
who enthusiastically and generously helped
in every possible way.

THE tiny truths
ILLUSTRATED BIBLE

CREATED BY: JOANNA RIVARD & TIM PENNER

OLD TESTAMENT

NEW TESTAMENT

INTRODUCTION

You might already know some of the stories in the Bible. But did you know that the Bible is actually one (VERY) big story?

In fact, it's the biggest, most important story in the whole world!

Of course, when you look inside you'll find lots of little stories—stories about stars and storms, dangerous journeys and surprising rescues. You'll find stories about wise queens, disobedient kings, and brave shepherds.

And one VERY important shepherd-king.

You'll meet people who do incredible things and some who make terrible mistakes, because the Bible is also about second chances and being forgiven.

But all of these little stories together tell one big story—the story of God's GREAT love for his children.

And because God made you, this is your story too. It's the true story of who you are and what you were made for.

Some parts of the Bible are complicated (even for grown-ups), and it's always good to ask questions. But the most important bits are VERY simple …

The Bible tells us:

Who God is—the One who made everything and everyone.
Who we are—his children, whom he loves no matter what.
What we were made for—to love him and everyone else.

So as you read and explore this incredible story (and continue to explore it for the rest of your life!), remember that it is still being written every day, and that you're a part of it too.

THE OLD TESTAMENT

CREATION

This is where it all starts. The VERY beginning.

At the beginning of everything there was nothing.

Except God.

And God was full of love, full of joy, bursting with happiness and excitement and life.

In fact, there was so much love and joy in God that he wanted to share it.

So God spoke into the nothingness, and something amazing happened.

"Let's start with some light!"
God said. And light appeared.

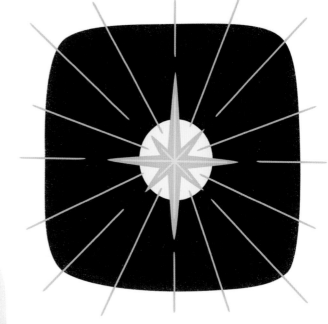

"Sky goes up here," he said,
"and oceans below."

God pulled land up from the
water to make tall mountains
and deep valleys. And he
covered them with plants
and trees.

"You are the sun," he said to a big light, placing it in the sky. "You'll light the day."

"You are the moon," he said to a smaller light. "You'll be our night-light."

"Oh, and stars too!" he said, and threw tiny lights across the dark sky.

God smiled.

"Beautiful!" he said.

And it was.

He filled the air with singing, flapping birds and all sorts of things that fly.

He filled the seas with splashing, leaping fish and all sorts of things that swim.

On land, he put all kinds of animals, from the wonderfully small to the magnificently tall.

Everything was bursting with life, and everything was just as it was made to be.

"Now, for the best part of all," said God. And he made a man and a woman to live with him in his perfect, beautiful world. They would be his—made to love him and be loved by him forever.

"You are my children," he said. "And this is ALL for you."

Then God stopped to look at everything he had made.

It was SO good. He smiled again, and then he rested.

The great story had begun!

ADAM AND EVE

God had made a wonderful garden for Adam and Eve, and in it they were wonderfully happy. It was the home they were made for, and they had everything they needed.

And God was with them in the garden.

God's garden was full of life. From the beautiful flowers to the towering trees, it was all theirs to explore, look after, and enjoy.

And everything would stay this way as long as Adam and Eve followed the one rule God had given them:

"You mustn't eat the fruit from this tree,"
God told them. "It will hurt you."

One day a crafty snake came to Eve in the garden—
he wanted to trick her.

"Did God really say, 'Don't eat any of the fruit in the garden'?"
the snake asked.

"Oh, no," said Eve. "There is only one tree we mustn't eat
from. God says the fruit will hurt us."

Eve knew that God loved her, and she trusted him. God
knew what was good for her and what was not. His rule was
meant to keep her safe.

But the snake told Eve a terrible lie.

"Oh, it's not going to hurt you," he said. "In fact, it will make
you just like God."

Then Eve wondered … did God really love her? Should she trust him?

Eve listened to the snake (who always tells lies) instead of trusting God (who always tells the truth).

She took the fruit and tasted it.

She gave some to Adam.

And then, because Adam and Eve had disobeyed God, EVERYTHING changed.

The world that God had made out of love was broken.

That night, God was walking in the garden in the cool evening air. He was looking for his beloved children.

"Where are you?" he called.

But Adam and Eve were hiding from God.

"Did you eat the fruit I told you not to eat?" God asked.
"Yes," said Adam. "It was Eve's fault."
"It was the snake's fault," said Eve.

Now God's heart was deeply sad, because his children had not trusted him.

God still loved Adam and Eve (they would always be his children), but the garden could no longer be their home. So he made clothes for them and sent them out.

Now sadness, sickness, and death had come into God's perfect world.

Everything was different.

But God wasn't any different. And his love wasn't different.

God didn't want his world to stay broken, and he didn't want his children to stay far from him. This wasn't what the world was made for, and it wasn't what his children were made for.

But God already had a plan—a plan to bring his children back to him.

One day everything would be made new again.

NOAH

Many years after Adam and Eve, there lived a man called Noah. Noah was God's friend. Noah remembered that he was one of God's children, but lots of people had forgotten they were God's children too. Because they didn't remember what God had made them for, they were hurting each other, hurting themselves, and hurting God.

This wasn't God's plan for his children. God doesn't like sadness, or hate, or hurting.

Something had to be done. And God wanted Noah to help him.

"Noah, I need you to build an ark," said God. (An ark is an enormous boat.)

"An ark?" asked Noah. "But there's no water around here."

"There will be soon," said God. "I'm going to send a flood to wash away everything that is bad in the world."

So right there, in the middle of a desert, far from any water, Noah began to build a boat.

It seemed crazy, but Noah trusted God.

When the ark was ready, God told Noah to fill it with animals— two of every kind he could find. When the animals and Noah's family had all squeezed inside, God closed the door.

Everyone waited. And then it started to rain. And rain. And rain.

Now Noah was glad he had listened to God.

It rained until the whole land was covered. As far as the eye could see, there was nothing but water.

But Noah—and everyone inside his boat—was safe.

Forty days and nights went by, and then one day, the rain stopped. Little by little, the water went down.

Slowly, dry land reappeared. Finally, Noah's ark came to rest on top of a mountain.

The huge doors opened, and Noah's family and all the animals stepped out into the fresh air. Up above them a rainbow stretched across the sky—a sign of God's promise that he would never do this again.

And when God makes a promise, he always keeps it.

ABRAHAM AND GOD'S PROMISE

Abraham was a friend of God, and like Noah, God spoke to him.

Abraham and his wife Sarah were old (really old), and sad because they had no children.

And now it was too late (or so they thought).

But God loved Abraham, and he had a big surprise for him.

It started with something small but would grow into something enormous—God's incredible plan for his family.

One night, Abraham and God were looking at the stars together.

"How many are there?" God asked.
"Far too many to count!" said Abraham.
"That's how many children and grandchildren and great-grandchildren (and great-great-great-great-grandchildren) I am going to give you," God told Abraham.

Abraham was very surprised. He and Sarah were far too old to be having children.

But God said, "Is anything impossible for me?" (The answer is no!)

God had something big in store—a promise that was going to stretch out just like the stars in the night sky above.

"I am going to give you a son," said God, "and a huge family. And through your family I will bless the WHOLE world."

"This is my promise to you," God told Abraham.

"I will always love you.
I will never leave you.
I will always look after you.

And one day I will give your family a beautiful land to call home. It will all start with your new son."

Abraham trusted God and believed him. When Sarah heard that she was going to be a mother, she laughed!

But God kept his promise and gave Abraham and Sarah a baby boy. They called him Isaac, which means "laughter," because God had kept the amazing, wonderful promise that had made Sarah laugh.

Abraham and Sarah's family grew and grew. This was the beginning of God's tribe. (A tribe is a group of people who live together and look after each other.)

God's special tribe would be different. It would be loved and loving. Its people would care because God cared for them.

Instead of only thinking about themselves, they would help others. Instead of worrying, they would trust God.

And through them God would bless other tribes, in all kinds of places.

Others would see that God was looking after his people and that he loved them and wanted them to be close to him.

JOSEPH

Abraham's tribe was beginning to grow.
Isaac grew up and had a son called Jacob.

Jacob had twelve sons, but one of them was his favorite.
His name was Joseph.

Jacob gave Joseph a very beautiful and special coat
because he loved him the most. Joseph's brothers were
upset. (They didn't have special coats.)

One night Joseph had a dream. He told his brothers, "I
dreamt I was like a prince, and you all bowed down to me."

Now Joseph's brothers hated him. Who did he think he was?
They wanted to get rid of Joseph and never see him again.
So they did.

One day they sold Joseph to some men for twenty silver coins.
The men took him a long way from home to a place called Egypt.

Then the brothers played a terrible trick on their father. They tore Joseph's special coat and showed it to Jacob.

A wild animal must have attacked him! he thought.

Jacob's heart was broken.

He thought he had lost his son forever.

Meanwhile, Joseph was alive (but things weren't going well for him).

He'd been taken from his home, made a slave, and thrown into prison for something he hadn't done.

But God was with Joseph, so Joseph trusted God and waited.

One night Pharaoh (the king of Egypt) had a strange and frightening dream. He dreamt that thin cows were eating fat cows. What did it mean? No one knew. But Pharaoh heard that Joseph could understand dreams. So he asked Joseph for help.

With God's help, Joseph explained the dream to Pharaoh. "A famine is coming and there will be nothing left to eat. We need to store food up now, while we have more than we need. Then later we will have enough."

Pharaoh was very grateful to Joseph and could see that he was wise. So he made him a prince and put him in charge of the whole country.

When the famine came, everyone in Egypt had enough food because they were prepared.

But Joseph's family, far away, had nothing left to eat. There was no food to be found anywhere. They were very hungry.

When Jacob heard that there was food in Egypt, he sent his sons to buy some.

Joseph's brothers had no idea that Joseph was there, at the palace. They didn't think they would ever see him again.

At first, the brothers didn't recognize Joseph and bowed down in front of him because he was now a prince. (Remember Joseph's dream?) But of course Joseph knew them. He still loved them and his heart was full of joy. "It's ME!" he said. "Your brother!"

Joseph's brothers were VERY surprised and a bit scared. They had treated him terribly, after all. But Joseph wasn't angry. He hugged them and forgave them.

"You see," he said, "God had a plan for my life. He brought me here to save lives and to save you."

Joseph brought his whole family to Egypt, and it grew and grew (just as God had promised Abraham it would).

A long time passed and Egypt had a new pharaoh. When he saw Joseph's family (God's tribe) growing, he was worried. There were so many of them. What if they wanted to take over his kingdom?

So Pharaoh came up with a plan ... and it wasn't good for God's people.

MOSES AND PHARAOH

God's tribe kept getting bigger. Pharaoh, the king of Egypt, was worried it was getting too big. He wanted to keep them under control, so he made them his slaves and forced them to work for him.

Now life was very different for God's people. They had been happy and free but now they were tired, miserable, and trapped. Nothing changed for a long, long time.

But then, in the middle of their sadness, the people remembered that they belonged to God, and that he loved them and had promised to stay with them. So they called out to him and asked him to rescue them.

And God listened.

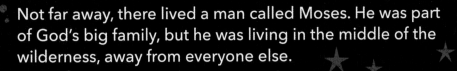

Not far away, there lived a man called Moses. He was part of God's big family, but he was living in the middle of the wilderness, away from everyone else.

One day Moses was looking after his sheep when he saw something strange. It was a bush on fire. But the bush wasn't burning up—it just kept on burning. As he got nearer, Moses heard a voice speaking to him.

It was coming from the bush!

"Moses!" said the voice.

"Yes?" said Moses.

"I am the God of your family—of Abraham, Isaac, and Jacob. My people have asked for my help. They want to escape from Egypt, and I am going to rescue them. I want you to go and tell Pharaoh to let them go."

"Oh, I can't do that," said Moses. "No way!"

Moses didn't think he was good enough to do the job. But God isn't afraid to use people who aren't perfect (and no one is perfect).

"Don't worry," said God. "I'll be with you."

So Moses trusted God and went to tell Pharaoh to let God's people go. Pharaoh was angry—he didn't want to lose all his slaves, after all.

"No!" Pharaoh said, and he gave God's people even more work to do.

But Pharaoh didn't know God, or what God could do.

"I will show Pharaoh that I am God," God told Moses, "and he will let my people go." So he sent all kinds of trouble to Egypt. Strange and unpleasant things started to happen.

First, God made the water in the river impossible to drink and all the fish in it died.

"Let my people go!" said Moses.
"No," said Pharaoh.

Then God sent a plague of frogs (which means a LOT of frogs) to Egypt. They came up out of the river and were EVERYWHERE!

"Let my people go!" said Moses.
"No," said Pharaoh.

So God sent huge clouds of flies to Egypt. They swarmed into the palace and filled every home.

"Let my people go!" said Moses.
"No," said Pharaoh.

God sent many plagues to the Egyptians. He sent more insects, he sent a horrible sickness to the Egyptians and all of their animals, and he sent the worst-ever hailstorm to destroy everything. Then he hid the sun and made it so dark that the Egyptians couldn't see anything at all.

And still Pharaoh said, "No!"

But God doesn't give up. Finally he sent so much trouble to Egypt that Pharaoh had no choice but to change his mind.

"Please go," he said.

So Moses and God's
people escaped from
Egypt just as God had promised.
They were no longer slaves. They were free!

They had called out to God and he had rescued them.

GOD RESCUES HIS PEOPLE

God's people were no longer slaves in Egypt. They were FREE! But where were they going and how would they get there?

This is how God showed them the way.

By day he put a huge cloud in the sky for them to follow. At night he put a huge fire in the sky to give them light and warmth. It was impossible to get lost. And they knew, day and night, that God was with them.

God's people followed the cloud and the fire until they came to a great sea where they set up their camp.

But back in Egypt, Pharaoh had changed his mind. Again! He wanted his slaves back.

Pharaoh was a strong king—he had a great army with lots of chariots and horses. And he knew that God's people were trapped by the sea. He thought it would be easy to catch them.

But he was wrong (because God was in charge).

God's people looked at the water in front of them and at Pharaoh's army behind them. There was no way out. Things looked impossible.

But *our* impossible things are not impossible for God.

"Moses, stretch your hand out over the water," God said.

And then something unbelievable happened! God sent a strong wind to blow and blow. The wind blew the water apart and made a dry path THROUGH the sea.

All God's children had to do was trust ... and keep going.

Pharaoh's army tried to follow them through the sea.

But as soon as God's people were safely across, God let all the water fall back again.

Now no one could catch God's people—not even Pharaoh with all his horses and chariots.

On that day God showed his people who he was and how much he loved them. And he gave them Moses to be their leader.

Then all of God's children celebrated, of course! They were really and truly, wonderfully free. They danced and they sang. They thanked God for being their rescuer.

Right there, God and his people were together again. They loved him and trusted him. They knew that he was good and that he was looking after them.

MOSES AND GOD'S RULES

God had rescued his people from Egypt.
Now they were out in the desert with no
place of their own. They needed a new home.

But God had already thought of that.

Remember God's promise to Abraham?
God had promised him an enormous family
AND a beautiful place for that family to live.

"I will give you everything you need,"
God told his people.

All God's people had to do was follow him from where they were (the hot, dry, dusty desert) to where he wanted them to be (somewhere wonderful, full of good things).

So off they set, walking through the desert. But as soon as they started to get hot and dirty and thirsty (which wasn't long at all), they started to grumble.

God's people were good at forgetting.

Sometimes they forgot all the good things God had done. Sometimes they forgot what he had promised. They forgot to trust him.

So they grumbled about being hot and complained about being tired. They thought God wasn't looking after them at all.

But he was. In the middle of the desert God took them to a special place with wonderful springs of fresh water to drink and cool, shady trees to sit under.

He was showing them how much he cared about them.

Soon God's people were grumbling again.

"Life in the desert is too hard," they complained. "What will we do when we have no more food?"

But God was looking after them.

One morning they woke up and found something called *manna* all over the ground. Moses told them that it was for making bread. Every morning they gathered just enough for the day.

So God's people kept traveling, and every day God made sure that they had what they needed.

One day God brought Moses and his people to a place called Mount Sinai. At the bottom of the mountain, they set up their camp. But this wasn't the land God had promised.

Why had they stopped?

Something important was going to happen here. God had good things in store for his family, and this was where he was going to tell them about it.

God told Moses to climb to the top of Mount Sinai. God was going to tell Moses how he wanted his people to live now that they were free.

So Moses climbed to the very top of the mountain. And there, surrounded by a thick cloud, God spoke to him. His voice was loud like thunder.

"I am your God who rescued you from Egypt. Never forget that. I am loving, faithful, and forgiving. If you obey my rules, I will do amazing things. Other tribes will see all that I do for you and will know who I am," God told Moses.

"You will be my treasured people."

God gave Moses ten special rules. He wrote them on stone tablets and Moses brought them back down the mountain.

God's ten special rules weren't the only instructions he gave to his people. There were LOTS more.

He wanted to teach them how to love him and love each other. He wanted them to be a different kind of tribe—just as he had told Abraham.

There were rules to teach them how to take care of neighbors from other tribes who were poor and needy.

There were rules to teach them to take
care of neighbors in their own tribe.

And there were rules to help them remember what God had
done for them so that they would keep trusting him and stay
close to him.

But the most important rule was this—to love God with all
their hearts and to love their neighbors too.

SPIES IN THE PROMISED LAND

God had given his people new rules for living, and now it was time for him to bring them to their new home—the land he had promised them.

As they got closer, they wondered: What would it be like? Would it be just as wonderful as God had said?

So God told Moses, "Send twelve men to explore the land." Moses sent the men off to find out everything they could about this new place.

 The spies crept quietly into the land and saw that it was INCREDIBLE! It was everything God had promised it would be.

There was just one problem—there were already people living in the land.

 And they were big. And they were scary.

The spies rushed back to tell everyone the news.
"This land is green and beautiful and full of delicious things to
eat—pomegranates and figs, and look at these gigantic grapes!"
It was far better than they had dreamed it would be.

"It's amazing," they said, "and everything is huge!"

"But so are the people who live there! There's no way we can get past them."

The spies were so scared that soon everyone else was scared too. In fact, they were terrified.

But wait! Not everyone was worried. Two of the spies were different. Caleb and Joshua trusted God because they remembered Egypt.

They remembered how God had rescued them.

They remembered that God keeps his promises.

Which meant ... this promised land would be theirs.

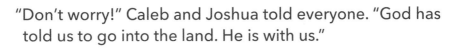

"Don't worry!" Caleb and Joshua told everyone. "God has told us to go into the land. He is with us."

But instead of obeying, God's people grumbled.

Instead of trusting in God's love, they were fearful.

They even wondered if life back in Egypt was better— working as Pharaoh's slaves!

Here they were, on the edge of the incredible land God had promised to give them. It was everything they needed. But instead of trusting God, they were questioning him.

God was not pleased. His own people had not trusted in his love.

Because they refused to go into his promised land, God sent the tribe back into the desert.

Few who were there that day would ever return.

But Joshua and Caleb would one day enter the promised land, because they had trusted God.

In fact, Joshua would become the new leader and he would lead God's people into their promised home.

God's plan for his people hadn't changed and neither had his love. One day he would give them another chance.

JERICHO

Joshua was the new leader of God's people. After many long years in the hot, dusty wilderness, God was giving his children a second chance to enter the land he had promised them.

This time they would obey him.

There was just one thing standing between them and their new home. Actually, it was rather a big thing. It was an ENORMOUS city called Jericho.

Joshua sent two men to spy on the city.

The king of Jericho heard that there were spies in his city and he sent soldiers to catch them.

The spies needed help.

In Jericho there lived a brave woman called Rahab. She had heard stories about God and believed they were true. She wanted to help God's people.

Rahab knew that the king was trying to catch the two spies, so she did something very dangerous—she hid them on the roof of her house.

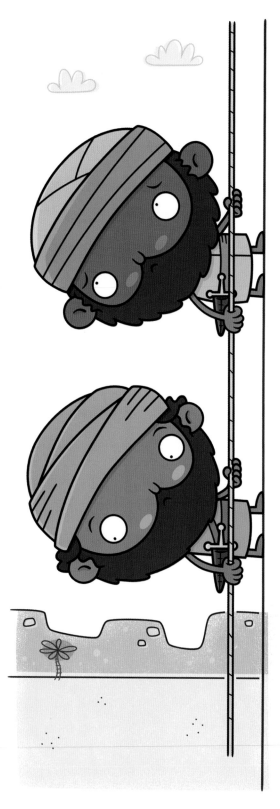

When night came, the spies climbed down the city walls and escaped.

The king's soldiers looked everywhere for them. The people of Jericho were frightened of God's tribe because they knew that God was strong.

Rahab asked for God's protection. The spies promised her that she would be safe because she had shown them kindness.

And because Rahab trusted God, he kept her and her family safe.

The two spies rushed back to Joshua and told him what they had heard.

"The people of Jericho are terrified of us because they have heard how God rescued us from Egypt and made a dry path through the Red Sea."

"They've heard how God has helped us defeat our enemies. They say that our God is the supreme God of the heavens above and the earth below."

"No one wants to fight us!"

Jericho wasn't just a huge city. It was a fortress (which means it had high walls, enormous gates, and no easy way to get in or out). This was the strongest city God's people had ever seen.

Getting in, through, over, or past it seemed impossible.

But God had a different plan. He told his people to march around the city once a day for six days. No charging, no shouting, no battle cry. Just the sound of their trumpets.

This wasn't how they usually fought their battles. This wasn't how ANYONE fought a battle.

But this time they trusted God and did what he asked.

Inside the city walls, the people of Jericho trembled and wondered what was happening.

After six days, God told his people to march around the city seven times. This time the trumpets blasted and everyone shouted as loudly as they possibly could.

And then ... something very surprising happened.

The strong, tall walls of Jericho came crashing down.

All of them.

Because God had helped his people, and because they had trusted him, Jericho was no longer in their way.

Now, at last, God's people could enter their new home, their promised land.

God had promised Abraham a special tribe and a new home. He had rescued his people from Egypt and given them freedom. He had kept them safe in the desert and given them food and water. He had given them rules to teach them to live well.

And now he had given them a new home.

They were just where God wanted them to be.

KING SAUL

God's people had a beautiful new home. God had kept his promise and he was taking care of them.

But even though they had EVERYTHING they needed, they looked around and noticed that other tribes had something they didn't.

Other tribes had kings. They wanted a king too.

"We want a king!" they said to Samuel. (By that time, Samuel was their leader, and God often spoke to him.)

But God knew that they didn't need a king—they only needed him. (Remember that God had told Abraham that his tribe was going to be different? They were never meant to be like everyone else.)

"I rescued you from Egypt," said God. "Remember? You are my people! I am already your king."

But God's tribe wanted to be like all the other tribes.

"I will give them a king," God told Samuel. "But he will not look after you the way I do."

So God chose a king. His name was Saul.

At first, Saul was a good king.

But soon he started to care more about his own plans than God's plans. He stopped trusting God.

And then he stopped obeying him.

This made God sad. He had told his people that they didn't need this kind of king—HE was their king.

But God always has a plan to make things right again.

So God decided to choose a new king for his people—a king who would love him with all his heart.

DAVID AND GOLIATH

As God was looking for a new king, he saw David—
a shepherd who loved him with all his heart.

David didn't have an important job and he wasn't a prince.
He wasn't even big or strong.

But he was a good shepherd. And sometimes a good
shepherd makes a good king.

One day David was out in the fields looking after his sheep.

God told Samuel to visit David's family. He was going to show Samuel who the new king would be.

One by one David's father, Jesse, brought his sons to Samuel. They were all big and strong. Who would God choose?

But one by one Samuel said, "No, not him."

"Is there anyone else?" he asked.

"Well, there is David," said Jesse, "but he's the youngest and the smallest."

"Bring him to me!" said Samuel.

So David was brought in from the fields.

"He is the one!" God told Samuel.

God had chosen a shepherd boy to become the next king, a king who would serve his people and serve God.

Not long after that, a tribe called the Philistines wanted to fight God's people.

They had a big and scary army. And one of their men was ESPECIALLY big and scary. His name was Goliath. He looked like a giant and he liked fighting. Goliath was taunting God's family and he was taunting their God. Goliath wanted a fight.

But no one wanted to fight him (he was FAR too big).

But David wasn't scared.

In fact, he was angry that Goliath was making fun of God.

"I'll fight him," he said. "When I'm out in the fields with my sheep, bears and lions come to attack us, and with God's help I fight them off. If God has protected me from the claws of lions and bears, he will protect me from this giant."

David took five little stones and his sling and walked toward Goliath.

Goliath looked at him and laughed.

But Goliath didn't know David's God.

"You have your sword and your spear," said David, "but I have God to help me."

David took just one stone and flung it at Goliath. The stone hit him right in the forehead, and he fell to the ground. The fight was over.

That day God's people defeated the Philistine army because God was with them.

David became a great king and a great hero to God's people. He wasn't a perfect king or a perfect person, but he loved God and he tried to follow God's rules.

David was called "a man after God's heart," which means that his heart loved God more than anything else.

David understood that God's people needed to be close to God, where he could help them and protect them. He knew that they were made to love God and trust in his promises.

KING SOLOMON

King David was getting old and it was time for a new king to lead God's people. David chose his son Solomon and everyone celebrated, hoping that he would be an even greater king than David.

God loved Solomon very much. And he had some surprising, incredible things in store for him.

One night God spoke to Solomon in a dream. "Ask me for anything you want," he said, "and I will give it to you."

What would Solomon ask for? Lots of money? A palace? A thousand horses? No. Solomon asked for wisdom (wisdom means knowing what is right and true). Why? Solomon wanted to be wise so that he could be a good king for God's people.

This made God happy. Because Solomon had chosen wisdom instead of money or power or a long life, God promised to give him ALL of those things.

God kept his promise to Solomon, and Solomon became incredibly wise and amazingly rich. In fact, he became the wisest king in the world. When people had problems or arguments, they came to him and he had the answer. Nothing was too tricky for him.

This made him a very good king.

And because he loved God, Solomon built a huge, beautiful temple where everyone could worship God and thank him. Then he built himself an enormous, fancy palace. His kingdom grew, and people from far and wide heard about his riches, his power, and his wisdom.

One day the queen of Sheba, who lived far away, heard about King Solomon and came to see his kingdom for herself. She was curious; was he really as wise and as rich as she had heard?

When she arrived she saw that everything she had heard about Solomon and his kingdom was true.

"I can see that God is great," she told him, "and that he has given you incredible gifts. But remember," she said, "God wants you to be a fair and good king. It is your job to show God's people the right way to live.

"God has given you all this so that you can serve others."

But as Solomon grew older, he started to love God less and love his money and power more. He no longer loved God with his whole heart.

Instead of trusting God to look after his people, he stored up gold and riches for himself. Instead of trusting God to protect his people, he built a huge army. He even used slaves to build himself a bigger kingdom.

Do you remember when God's people were slaves in Egypt? God had rescued them so that they could be free and could live differently as his special children.

But now, instead of blessing other tribes, they were using them as slaves to make their kingdom bigger. This wasn't part of God's plan.

Solomon had forgotten what God had made him for.

God's heart was sad again, and he took everything away from Solomon.

Many kings came after Solomon. Some of them loved God, but most did not. Over and over again God's people forgot how to love him with all their hearts. They forgot how to follow God and they stopped obeying his rules. They forgot what they were made for.

Because of that, God allowed his people to be taken away from the promised land—the special home he had given them.

They found themselves far away, captive in a place called Babylon.

But even in this new place, God was still with them. He had a plan to bring them back to where they belonged and to make things right again.

DANIEL AND THE LIONS

God's people were far from home, in a kingdom called Babylon. But God hadn't forgotten about them—he hadn't left them. And even though the people of Babylon didn't know God, they knew there was something different about God's people.

In fact, King Darius (the king over Babylon) had noticed someone very special in God's tribe.

His name was Daniel. Daniel knew God and he loved him. God had made Daniel very clever and very wise.

The king saw this and wanted to put Daniel in charge of the whole kingdom. It was a very important job.

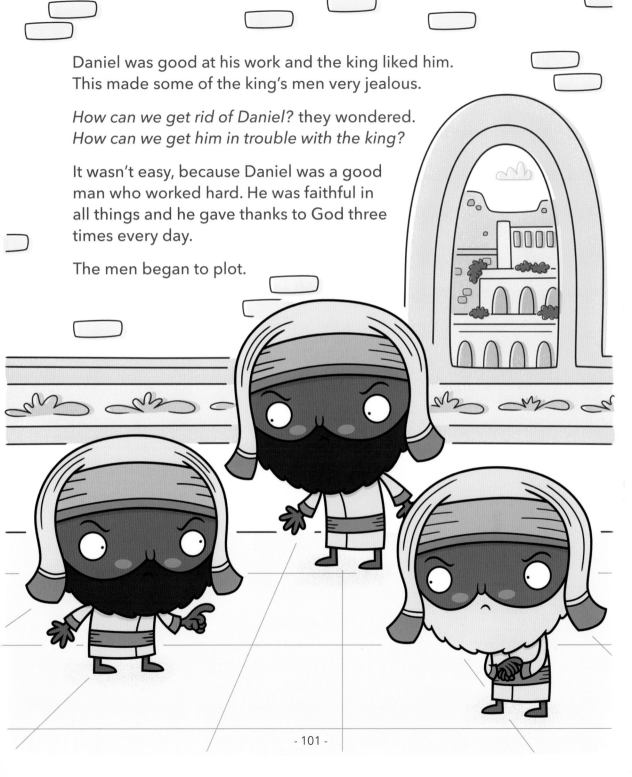

Daniel was good at his work and the king liked him. This made some of the king's men very jealous.

How can we get rid of Daniel? they wondered. *How can we get him in trouble with the king?*

It wasn't easy, because Daniel was a good man who worked hard. He was faithful in all things and he gave thanks to God three times every day.

The men began to plot.

When the men saw that Daniel prayed to God three times a day, they had an idea.

They would trick the king and get rid of Daniel forever.

The men went straight to King Darius.

"We need a new law," they told him. "Because you are such a wise and wonderful king, everyone must pray to you and to no one else. If anyone disobeys, you must throw them into the lions' den!"

The king liked this law (he didn't know they were tricking him), so he said yes.

It wasn't long before Daniel heard about the new law. But it didn't stop him. He trusted God, so he kept praying to him.

When the king's men saw Daniel asking God for help, they rushed off to tell the king.

"Daniel is praying to his God!" they said. "You must throw him to the lions because he's breaking your new law."

King Darius realized he had been tricked and his heart was sad.

He liked Daniel, and he didn't want him to be hurt. But there was nothing he could do—even he couldn't change the law.

The king's men took Daniel and dropped him into the den full of hungry lions.

"I hope that your God, who you love, will rescue you!" said the king.

So Daniel was left alone with the lions and the king went home. But the king was so worried about his friend that he didn't sleep at all.

The minute the sun came up, he rushed to the lions' den. "Daniel!" he shouted. "Has your God rescued you from the lions?"

The king heard ...
a voice!

"God has kept me
safe!" shouted
Daniel. "He sent an
angel to keep the
lions' mouths shut
all night!"

The king was overjoyed!

"Quickly! Get Daniel out of the lions' den!" he ordered.

After a whole night surrounded by fierce and rather hungry lions, there wasn't a single scratch on Daniel. Daniel had trusted God and God had kept him safe.

(As for the men who had tricked the king, well, they were in big trouble.)

Because of what God had done, King Darius made a new law:

Everyone in my kingdom must pray only to Daniel's God.

He is the true, living God who lives forever. His kingdom will last forever.

He is a rescuing God, who looks after his people.

And he has saved Daniel from the lions.

JONAH AND THE BIG FISH

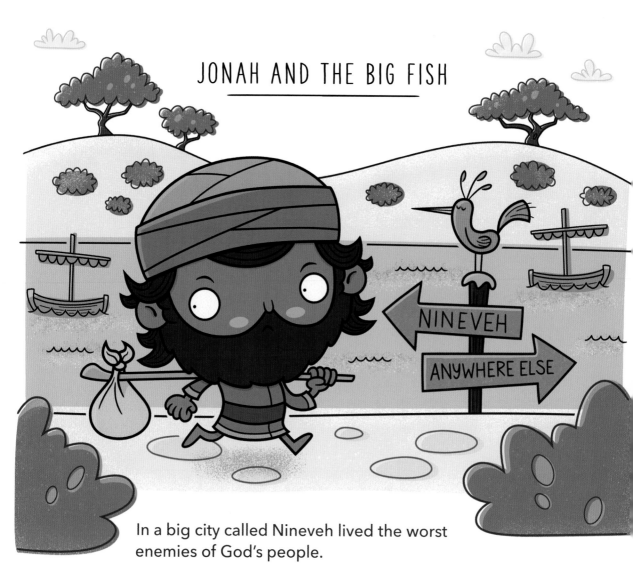

In a big city called Nineveh lived the worst enemies of God's people.

"Jonah," said God, "go to Nineveh and tell everyone to stop all the bad things they are doing. Tell them to say sorry and choose love instead."

But Jonah did NOT want to go. These people were his enemies. How on earth could God love THEM?

So Jonah jumped on a ship going away from Nineveh. He was trying to escape from God.

But God sent a dangerous storm over the sea. The terrified sailors on the boat prayed to their gods to save them. Nothing happened.

"It's my fault," said Jonah. "I'm running away from God. Throw me into the sea and the storm will stop."

So they did—and the storm stopped!

The sailors saw that Jonah's God was the only true God, and thanked him for rescuing them.

Meanwhile, God sent an enormous fish to swallow Jonah up.

Jonah's plan to run away from God was not going well. After three days stuck inside the fish, he realized he had made a mistake. He prayed to God, and God told the fish to spit him out.

"Now will you go?" God asked him.

This time, Jonah went straight to Nineveh and gave them God's message:

"God loves you, but he doesn't like the way you are living. It's not what he made you for. He made you for something better. Say sorry, and choose love."

And do you know what? The people listened. Even the king listened and was sorry. He took off his royal clothes and put on a dirty, itchy sack instead. Then he announced to his people, "Everyone in Nineveh must say sorry to God. We must love him and change our lives."

Jonah was shocked.

HOORAY!

The worst enemies of God's people had said
they were sorry and changed their ways.
What an amazing, happy ending!

But Jonah didn't think so. He was angry. He couldn't
understand why God loved these people. He didn't
want to share God's love with other tribes.

But God's love is bigger than that. His love is for
everyone—even enemies.

God's love is SO big that he never gives up on his children, no matter what.

Now God's people were scattered far from each other with no home of their own. (Remember that they had been taken from their land?)

They had no king of their own to look after them. And no idea how God was going to rescue them.

But God knew. He hadn't forgotten his children, or his plan for them. He was going to send them a very different kind of king.

A king who would show them just how big God's love is!

THE NEW TESTAMENT

THE FIRST CHRISTMAS

God's people had been scattered and were far apart (a bit like the stars in the sky above Abraham).

They didn't have a land of their own, and they didn't have a king who looked after them.

God had told them that he would send them a rescuing king. He loved them and wouldn't give up on them.

So here they were, waiting for a powerful rescuer who would be strong and battle their enemies for them.

But God had a very different idea.

This king wasn't going to be at all what they were expecting.

He would be so much MORE!

It all started when an angel visited Mary.

Mary was an ordinary girl who was going to marry a man named Joseph. They were going to have an ordinary life. Or so she thought.

"Mary," said the angel, "God has chosen you to have a baby who will change the world. He is God's son."

This came as a big surprise.

But Mary loved God and trusted him, so she said yes. "I will do whatever God wants," she said.

Not long afterward, just as the angel had said, Mary found that she was pregnant.

When the baby was about to be born, Mary and Joseph had to go on a long journey. The emperor had sent everyone back to their hometowns to be counted. Joseph was from King David's town, Bethlehem.

Remember good King David? He and Joseph were from the same family!

So off to Bethlehem went Joseph, Mary, and the soon-to-be-born baby.

The little town was packed full of visitors, and Joseph and Mary needed somewhere to stay—somewhere for Mary to have the baby.

When they found a place, it wasn't fancy. In fact, it was the place where the animals slept. But there, with the sheep, the goats, and the donkeys, the baby was born.

The promised baby. The one the angel had told Mary about.

And the name they gave him was Jesus!

God had sent his son to be born as a tiny little baby. And Jesus was going to change everything. This was the biggest, most glorious news in the world.

Who would God tell first? A king, or perhaps a queen?

No!

God told a group of shepherds. They were poor and dirty and nobody thought they were very important. They were out in the fields watching their sheep and minding their own business.

But all of a sudden ...

ANGELS appeared! The sky was full of them! They were bright, beautiful, and terrifying all at once. They had important news:

"A baby has been born!" they shouted. "He is God's son. He will bring great joy to the whole world. God is glorious, great, and wonderful!"

The shepherds knew exactly what to do. Leaving their sheep behind, they ran as fast as they could to find the baby. And there he was, exactly where the angels had said he would be.

Once they had seen him, they rushed to tell everyone what had happened and what the angels had told them.

This baby was God's Son and he would be the rescuing king!

Back in the fields, they sang songs to God, telling him how amazing he was.

When Jesus was born, a special star
appeared in the night sky.

Far away from Bethlehem,
three wise men (called Magi) saw
the star and knew what it meant.
They had been waiting, just like
God's people.

Now that the waiting was over
they wanted to see this new king.
So they set out on a long journey,
following the star that would take
them to Jesus.

When they found him at last, the Magi were overjoyed. They gave him special gifts—gold, frankincense, and myrrh—and bowed down because they knew who he was.

You see, they knew that he was the special king God's people had been waiting for. The one that God had promised to send.

The new king had finally arrived.

JOHN THE BAPTIST

This is John the Baptist.

John lived in the wilderness (a place outside the city where wild animals live). He made his own clothes out of camel hair (itchy!) and ate honey and locusts (locusts are like grasshoppers and are delicious with honey).

God had given John a very important job. He was telling everyone about Jesus (who had grown up by this time) and getting people ready for him.

Crowds came from far and wide to listen to John the Baptist because he was teaching something exciting. He told the people about loving God and living life with him, and how to say sorry for the things they had done wrong.

John reminded them that God had made them to love others, and told them to share their food and their clothes with people who didn't have enough.

He also dipped people in the river to show that they were starting a new life with God (this is called baptizing).

One day, as John was baptizing
people in the Jordan River, he
saw Jesus walking toward him.

"There he is!" John shouted, "the one I have been telling you about!
He has come to change us and rescue us. The whole world will be
different because of him."

"John, I want you to baptize me," Jesus told him.
"Me, baptize YOU?" John said.
"Yes!" said Jesus.

When John had baptized Jesus in the river, God's spirit came down to Jesus like a dove.

"You are my beloved son," God said, "and my great joy."

Jesus was now ready to begin the work that God had given him.

JESUS' DISCIPLES

Jesus was ready to begin what he had come to do. But first he needed a special group of friends to travel with him, to help him, and to learn from him. They would be his disciples.

Who would he choose? You might be surprised.

Simon, Andrew, James, and John were fishermen. Jesus met them down by the water one day while they were putting their fishing nets away.

"Let's go fishing!" Jesus said.

"We've been out all night," they told him, "and we didn't catch a single fish."

But because Jesus had asked them to, they dropped their nets back into the water. And straight away something amazing happened.

The fishermen could hardly believe their eyes. Their nets were so full of fish that their boats began to sink!

This was impossible! How had Jesus done this? They could tell there was something very different about this man.

"Come with me!" Jesus said. "I want you to be my disciples. I have a different job for you."

So the fishermen left everything by the water and followed him.

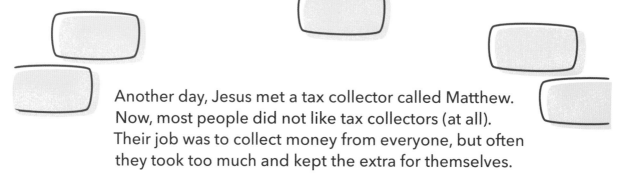

Another day, Jesus met a tax collector called Matthew.
Now, most people did not like tax collectors (at all).
Their job was to collect money from everyone, but often
they took too much and kept the extra for themselves.

Everyone knew this was NOT FAIR!

Matthew was a tax collector like all the others, but Jesus
knew that and loved him anyway. He had something
better for him.

"Come with me," Jesus said, "and be my disciple!"

So Matthew did.

Matthew was so happy that he threw a huge party at his house and invited Jesus and all his tax collector friends too.

But not everyone was pleased about Jesus' new friends. Why was he spending time with those types of people?

"Because," said Jesus, "these are the people who need me—the ones I have come to help."

Jesus wasn't doing things the way anyone expected. He made friends with all kinds of people. He cared about everyone because they were all God's children. And he loved them.

Jesus chose twelve disciples. For the next few years they would follow him wherever he went—near and far—learning, teaching, helping, and healing.

Jesus' disciples weren't perfect—sometimes they made mistakes, and sometimes they didn't understand everything he was saying.

But Jesus is forgiving and patient and can work with anyone.

He had come to change the world and show God's love to everyone. And he had chosen this unusual collection of people to help him.

THE SERMON ON THE HILL

Jesus began to teach people and tell them stories about living life with God. Wherever he went, people came to listen to him because his stories were different.

He was a different kind of teacher.

You see, when Jesus told stories, he was telling people all about God (what he is like and what he loves) and all about themselves (who they were and what they were made for).

One day Jesus sat on a hillside
and a crowd gathered around him.
He began to talk to them about their lives ...

"Look at the little birds and the beautiful flowers
around us," he said.

"Do you think they worry about what to wear, or
what to eat? Of course not! And neither should
you, because God made you and he loves you. He
knows just what you need.

"So don't worry about tomorrow. Be thankful for
what you have today."

"Now, sometimes we are sad. Sometimes other people hurt us, and sometimes we don't have the things we need," Jesus told them.

"But when life is hard, God is still with you.

"And when we feel sad, or broken, God is close to us— he does not leave us no matter what happens.

"And he will never stop loving us."

"If you love me," Jesus explained, "and love God, people will notice that your life looks different. You'll be like a bright light shining out to everyone. A light everyone can see. A light to show people the way.

"You'll be like a city high on a hill that everyone can see.

"When you do good things, people will see that God is good.

"When you are loving and kind, when you forgive others, when you make peace, you are living the way God made you to live."

"Remember the rules God gave to Moses?" Jesus asked them.

"I want to teach you to go even further. To love more!

"It's easy to love your friends. I want you to love your enemies.

"Pray for the people who hurt you.

"And when someone hurts you, don't hurt them back. Be kind!
  Forgive them.

"If someone asks you for something, give it to them.

"If someone takes your shirt, give them your jacket too.

"Show extravagant, surprising love! That's what God made you for."

It isn't easy to live this way. By ourselves, it would be impossible!
  But we have God as our Father and he loves to help us.

"And when you pray, this is how you can talk to God,"
 Jesus told them:

"Our Father in the heavens,
   your name is holy.
   May your kingdom come soon,
   and may what you want be done
   here on earth just like in heaven.
   Give us just what we need for today.
   Forgive us for the things we do wrong,
   and help us to forgive other people.
   Help us always to choose good,
   and keep us safe from evil.
   You are the king of everything, forever.
   All power everywhere belongs to you,
   and we will worship you always.

   Amen!"

JESUS CALMS A STORM

One night, Jesus and his friends were crossing a lake in a boat.

Jesus had spent all day helping people, and he was tired. Very soon, he fell asleep.

As Jesus was sleeping, a furious, wild storm swept across the lake.

Blustery winds and fierce waves threw the small boat around. Jesus' friends were terrified. They were sure their boat was going to sink.

"Wake up, Jesus!" they shouted.

"Save us! We're going to drown!"

Jesus opened his eyes and looked at their faces.

"Why are you so afraid?" he asked.
(You see, he knew they were perfectly safe with him.)

But his friends weren't feeling safe at all.

All they could see was the storm swirling around them.

Jesus stood up and spoke to the wind and the waves.

"Be quiet!"

That was all he said. And the wind and the waves listened.

They knew who he was. Everything was calm again.

The disciples were amazed and frightened too. After all, a storm had listened to Jesus and obeyed.

"Who is he?" they asked each other. "Even the wind and the waves do what he says."

The disciples were still learning who Jesus really was.

JESUS HEALS A LITTLE GIRL

Everywhere Jesus went, sick people came to him because they knew that he cared for them and could help them.

One day, Jesus was talking to a big crowd of people. A man called Jairus rushed up to him full of worry.

"My little girl is very, very sick," he said. "Please come and help her. I know you can make her well again."

Jesus wanted to help, so he went with Jairus to his house.

As they pushed through the busy crowds, a woman saw Jesus. She had been very sick for a long time and had heard Jesus could help.

If I can just touch his clothing, she thought, *I'll be better.*

Reaching through the crowd, she touched the edge of Jesus' cloak, and immediately knew that she was well again.

Jesus stopped. "Who touched me?" he asked.
"We're in the middle of a crowd!" said his disciples. "Everyone is touching you."

"It was me," the woman said.

Jesus smiled at her. "You don't need to be afraid," he said. "You are healed because you believed."

At that very moment some men arrived from Jairus' house. "It's too late," they told Jairus. "Don't bother the teacher anymore." But Jesus said to Jairus, "Don't be afraid. Trust me."

Jesus took Peter, James, and John into Jairus' house. He took the little girl's hand and said, "Little girl, get up."

The little girl opened her eyes and stood up. She was completely well!

"She's hungry," said Jesus. "Let's give her something to eat."

This was the happiest day of Jairus' life! Because he had believed in Jesus, his daughter had been healed.

JESUS HELPS AND HEALS

As Jesus was leaving Jairus' house, two blind men started
to follow him.
"Help us, Jesus!" they called.
Jesus stopped. "Do you think I can heal you?" he asked.
"Yes, Lord," they said.

So Jesus touched their eyes. "Because you believed, you
won't be blind anymore," he told them.

The two men opened their eyes and ... they could see!
Jesus had healed them.

Everywhere he went, Jesus loved the people no one else loved and cared for people no one else would go near.

Some people had a disease so horrible they were sent to live outside the city, away from everyone else. People were afraid of them.

But not Jesus. He loved them just as much as he loved everyone else, and he healed them when they asked him to.

He gave them new life.

More and more people heard about Jesus and the amazing, wonderful things he was doing. And more and more people came to ask for his help.

One day Jesus was at a house, and a huge crowd gathered around him. A group of friends arrived carrying a man who couldn't walk. They wanted Jesus to help their friend, but the house was so full of people that it was impossible to get in.

They were desperate to see Jesus because they knew he was the only one who could help. So they came up with an idea.

They climbed up to the top of the house, smashed a hole in the roof, and lowered their friend down ...

Right in front of Jesus.

Jesus looked at the man on the mat. "All the things you have done wrong are forgiven," he said, "and because your friends had faith, you are healed. Now get up and walk again."

And the man did! He stood up, picked up his mat, and walked home full of thanks to God.

Jesus knew that it was far more important to be forgiven than healed. But he also knew that the man wanted to walk again.

Because he loved the man, he did both: Jesus forgave him *and* healed him.

FEEDING 5000 (at least)

Jesus and his disciples had been traveling and teaching, helping and healing. One day, though, they needed to escape the crowds and rest. They set off across the lake, looking for a quiet spot. But when they reached the other side of the lake, they saw a huge crowd of people waiting for them—there were thousands of people!

Jesus could have turned around or told everyone to go home, but he looked out at his followers, loved them, and wanted to help them.

Jesus spent the whole day teaching and helping the enormous crowd. When evening came, everyone was hungry.

"There's no food here," the disciples said to Jesus. "Let's send everyone home."

"Why don't you feed them?" Jesus said.

"That's impossible!" they said. "How on earth could we buy food for all these people?"

"Show me what you have," Jesus said.

Well, all they had was one small meal from one small boy—just five loaves and two fish.

One tiny picnic for such an enormous crowd?

How ridiculous.

But Jesus gave
thanks to God and
broke the bread
and fish into pieces.

Jesus handed the food to the disciples and told them to pass it out. So off they went, thinking, *This isn't nearly enough! Any minute now, we'll run out.*

But they didn't. No matter how much food they gave away, they still had more. And everyone ate until they couldn't manage another crumb.

When the disciples had picked up all the leftovers, they had twelve full baskets.

Jesus had given the people even more than they needed.

Night was coming, so Jesus sent the crowds and the disciples home. But he went up into the hills to pray.

ZACCHAEUS

Zacchaeus was an important tax collector and he was very rich.
His job was collecting money from everyone.
But (like most tax collectors) he often took
too much and kept it for himself.

Most people didn't like tax
collectors, and plenty of people
didn't like Zacchaeus.

One day Zacchaeus heard that Jesus was coming to his town.

Everyone seemed to be talking about this man and the amazing things he was doing.

Zacchaeus was curious—he wanted to see Jesus too.

So off he went.

But Zacchaeus wasn't the only one who wanted to see Jesus that day.

And unfortunately for Zacchaeus, he couldn't see over the crowds. (He just wasn't tall enough.)

This was a problem.

So Zacchaeus came up with an idea. He scrambled up into the branches of a nearby tree and watched for Jesus.

All of a sudden he spotted him! He couldn't believe what he was seeing—Jesus was walking right toward him.

"Hello, Zacchaeus," said Jesus. "I want to come to your house today. Come down from up there."

Well, that wasn't at all what Zacchaeus had expected. In fact, it wasn't what anyone had expected. Why was Jesus visiting a tax collector?

Everyone knew what Zacchaeus was like. And, of course, so did Jesus.

But he loved him all the same. Zacchaeus leapt down from his branch, overjoyed that Jesus wanted to come to HIS house.

And because he could tell that Jesus really loved him, Zacchaeus wanted to change, right then and there.

"I want to make things right again," he told Jesus. "I'm going to give away half of everything I have. And if I've stolen from anyone, I'll give them back four times as much."

Zacchaeus had been given a new life, which is what Jesus came to do—love the people others didn't and bring everyone close to him.

THE LOST SHEEP

Jesus liked to tell stories. He used them to teach people about God.

One day Jesus was with a group of people who didn't have many friends and weren't at all popular. They had stolen money, cheated others, hurt people, and made enemies.

This bothered some people (why was Jesus friends with THAT crowd?).

So Jesus told this story ...

Once there was a shepherd who had one hundred sheep.

He loved them all and took very good care of them. He knew that the best place for them was close to him. Every night when the sun went down, he counted his sheep carefully, making sure they were all safe.

But one night the shepherd counted to ninety-nine. And then stopped. One of his precious sheep was missing. This was awful. The worst!

There was only one thing to do.

He HAD to find his lost sheep. Off he rushed, leaving the others behind.

He searched high.

He searched low.

All through the night he hunted, worried about his one precious sheep.

Then, at last, he saw him! He grabbed that little sheep and carried him all the way home.

And oh how happy he was—how full of joy! His precious sheep was back where he belonged.

"I am the shepherd," Jesus said, "and you are my sheep. The best place for you is close to me, because you are mine.

"Just like the shepherd who celebrated when he found the lost sheep, God is full of joy whenever one of his children comes home to him."

THE PRODIGAL SON

This is another story Jesus told about what God is like:

Once there was a man who had two sons. The youngest son wanted to leave home. He wanted to be far from his father and brother and do whatever he liked. So he went to his father and said, "Father, give me half of your money. I want to leave home."

The father was surprised and sad. After all, this was a very hurtful thing to ask.

But he divided his money in two, gave it to his sons, and the younger son left.

The son went far away and lived the life that he wanted. He bought lots of things, threw lots of parties, and made lots of friends.

He wasted his money.

He didn't think much about his father or about life back home.

But one day all the money was gone. He had spent everything! Soon all his friends were gone too.

Now he had ... nothing. A famine came and the son was desperate for food. He found a job feeding pigs (which was the WORST job he could imagine). He was so hungry he wished he could eat the pigs' food.

And then, surrounded by those dirty, smelly pigs, he remembered something—his father's house.

Even my father's servants have food to eat, he thought.
*I will go home, say sorry, and ask my father to give me a job.
Then I can eat again.*

He set off on the long journey home. But when his father saw him in the distance, the old man ran to him.

You see, he had been waiting for his son.

The father threw his arms around him, hugged him, and kissed him—he simply could not hide his love.

"Father, I'm sorry—" the son started to say, but his father didn't let him finish. He was bursting with joy and excitement.

"Quickly," the father shouted to his servants, "get me a special robe for my boy! Prepare a huge feast for the whole neighborhood. We are having a party!

"My son was lost, and now he is home."

The older brother heard the music and dancing and wondered what all the fuss was about. When he heard that the party was for his brother, he was angry.

"I've worked hard for you my whole life," he said to his father, "and you have never thrown a party like this for me."

"My son," said the father, "you are always with me and everything I have is yours. But now is the time to celebrate because your brother was gone and now he is home. He is back where he belongs."

THE GOOD SAMARITAN

Another day, a man who knew a lot about the rules God had given to Moses came to Jesus with a question.

"How does God want us to live?" he asked.

"What does the Bible say?" Jesus asked him.

"Love God with all your heart, with all your soul, with all your mind, and with all your strength," said the man. "And love your neighbor the way you love yourself."

"That's right," said Jesus.

"But who is my neighbor?" asked the man.

So Jesus told him a story ...

A man was traveling from Jerusalem to Jericho. The journey was long and the road was dangerous. All of a sudden, he was attacked by a group of men. They took everything he had and hurt him badly.

The men ran off and left him lying on the side of the road, too injured to walk.

As he lay there, a man came along. He was a priest—and had spent his whole life obeying God's rules. Surely he would stop and help?

No! He kept walking.

Soon someone else came along. He was a Levite—someone who also knew all about God's rules, and how God wants us to help people. Surely he would stop?

No! He walked right past the man who needed his help.

Finally, another man came along. He was a Samaritan. God's people did not like the Samaritans AT ALL. A Samaritan would never stop to help. He couldn't be the hero of this story.

Could he?

The Samaritan saw the wounded man and saw that he needed help. So he stopped. He washed the man's wounds and bandaged him up.

Then he put him on his own donkey, brought him to an inn (a place where he could stay), and took care of him.

The next day he gave the innkeeper some money. "Look after him," he said. "When I come back, I will pay for the rest."

"Who was a neighbor to the man who needed help?" Jesus asked.

"The one who took care of him," said the man.

"Then go and be like him!" said Jesus.

Jesus told this story to show people how to love. When God tells us to love our neighbor, he means ... everyone.

The Samaritan loved the person who hated him. That was extravagant and surprising love.

Because God's love is big, ours should be too.

That's how God wants us to live.

JESUS LOVES KIDS

Everywhere Jesus went, crowds would come to him, and he would teach them and help them. One day while he was teaching, some people brought their children to meet him. They wanted Jesus to pray for them and bless them.

The disciples tried to stop them. They thought that Jesus was too busy to spend time with little kids.

But Jesus didn't think like that. He LOVED children!

"Come!" he said, with his arms open wide.

The children ran to him (they knew what they were made for).

"Don't stop them," Jesus said to his friends.

"God's kingdom is for everyone. It's a gift. And the only thing you need to do is come.

"Just like these little ones."

Then he took them in his arms and blessed them.

JESUS' LAST DAYS

All over the city of Jerusalem, God's people were preparing for an important feast called Passover.

Remember when God rescued his people from Egypt? Every year they shared a special meal together, remembering and celebrating what God had done for them. They didn't want to forget.

So Jesus came back to Jerusalem to celebrate with his friends.

As he entered the city, a big crowd welcomed Jesus like a king— they were starting to see who he really was (the king they had been waiting for) and what he had come to do (rescue them).

But not everyone thought that Jesus was a king. And not everyone was excited about him. In fact, some important leaders were very angry that so many people were following Jesus.

These men didn't want people to listen to Jesus—they wanted everyone to listen to them and follow their rules.

"He isn't a king," they said, "and we need to stop him."

So they made a plan.

Judas, one of Jesus' disciples, agreed to help them. In return they gave him a bag of silver coins.

On the night of the big feast, Jesus was with his disciples.

Before the disciples could sit and eat, their feet needed to be washed. After walking through the dusty, dirty city streets, they were filthy.

Washing dirty feet was a servant's job (and not a very nice one), but suddenly Jesus knelt down and started to wash the disciples' feet. They were shocked!

"Stop!" they said. "You shouldn't do that! That's not your job!"

"But this is what it means to love one another," said Jesus.

"When we really, truly love each other, we serve one another." Jesus was surprising his disciples again.

Jesus knew that he didn't have much time left with his friends.

As they sat together, Jesus said to them, "I want you to love each other the way I have loved you."

He thanked God for their meal and they shared it together.

"When I'm gone, remember me," Jesus told them, "especially when you share bread and wine like this."

The disciples sat and listened to Jesus. But Judas left quietly and went out into the night alone.

Later that night, Jesus and some of his disciples went to a quiet place so that Jesus could pray. Jesus knew what was about to happen, and his heart was sad and afraid.

He wanted to talk to his Father, God.

"Stay here and pray," he told his disciples. Jesus walked a short distance away, knelt down, and prayed.

When he came back to his friends, he found them asleep. He was sad that they hadn't stayed awake with him.

"Wake up," he said. "It is time."

At that moment, Judas found Jesus and his disciples in the garden. An angry crowd was with Judas. This is what the leaders had paid Judas to do—to bring them to Jesus, away from the other people. They had come to arrest Jesus.

The disciples tried to stop them, but Jesus told them not to.

He knew that this was part of God's plan, and he refused to fight back. Instead, he let them take him away.

The very next day, Jesus was led to a place where criminals were taken, even though he was God's perfect Son who had never done anything wrong.

There, just outside the city, he allowed himself to be punished like a criminal, and then he died.

Which might have been the end of the story.

Except that it wasn't!

This was part of God's plan. Jesus' death would lead to new life for everyone. It would lead to restoration, which means making things right again.

It looked like a terrible ending. But it was actually an unbelievable new beginning.

JESUS COMES BACK

Later that day, Jesus' body was wrapped in a cloth and laid in a special place, called a tomb, in a garden.

An enormous stone was rolled in front of the tomb's door. Two guards stood by the stone so that no one could get in (or out).

Everything was dark.

Two days later, early in the morning, a group of women who loved Jesus went to the garden. They were sad because they thought this was the end of the story, and they wanted to see Jesus one more time.

As they walked, they wondered how they would be able to move the huge stone in front of the tomb.

"Who will roll it away for us?" they asked each other.

But when they arrived in the garden, they saw something they were not expecting.

Someone had moved the stone!

"Don't be afraid!" said a voice. There, on top of the enormous stone, was an angel.

"I know you are looking for Jesus. He is not here. He is alive again. Come and see!"

The women peered into the dark tomb.

It was empty!

They were overjoyed, amazed, and terrified all at once. Could Jesus really be alive? Was the story not over after all?

"You must go and tell his disciples," said the angel. So the women ran as fast as they could.

But suddenly, someone appeared right in front of them. It was the ONE person they had most wanted to see. It was Jesus. He really was alive!

They rushed to him.

"Lord!" they cried.

"Don't be afraid!" he said. "Go and tell my friends everything."

The disciples were hiding. They were sad that Jesus had died and frightened that they might be taken away too because they were his friends.

The women rushed in, bursting with excitement over their incredible news.

"Jesus is alive!" they shouted.

But the men didn't believe them.

Before long, Jesus himself appeared.

At first, the disciples were terrified—they thought he was a ghost!

"Don't be afraid of me!" he told them. "I'm not a ghost. Come, touch me and see. Give me something to eat. I'm hungry."

The disciples were full of joy and wonder. Jesus really was alive! They could hardly believe what was happening.

"You saw everything I did and heard what I taught you," Jesus said to them. "You've seen everything that has happened to me. Now I want you to go everywhere and tell everyone about it.

"Go and make new disciples—people like you who will love me and follow me.

"Tell everyone about my love and my forgiveness.

"Teach them to obey everything I have taught you—to live the way God wants you to live.

"And remember—I will always be with you wherever you go."

THE HOLY SPIRIT

Jesus spent a few more days with his disciples. But he knew that it would soon be time for him to leave them.

One day as they were sharing a meal, he told them, "Don't leave Jerusalem yet, because God has a special gift for you, a gift that you will need once I am gone.

"With this gift you will be able to go and tell everyone about me, here in Jerusalem and everywhere in the world. And you'll know that I'm still with you because of it."

It was finally time for Jesus to leave his friends. He had finished
everything he had come to do. As his disciples gathered around him,
Jesus was taken up into the sky until he was hidden by the clouds.

Suddenly, two men dressed in white appeared to the disciples.

"One day," they said, "you will see Jesus again—he will come back."

After Jesus had gone, the disciples spent lots of time together talking about Jesus and waiting for the gift that he had promised to give them.

What would it be?

Not long afterward they were together in a home when they heard a sound like a strong, rushing wind. It was so loud that it filled the whole house.

They looked at one another in surprise and saw flames of fire above their heads. What was happening? Jesus was keeping his promise—God was using the fire and the wind to show them that his Spirit had come and would always be with them. The Holy Spirit would be their helper, their comforter, and their guide. Just as Jesus had been.

At that time, people were visiting Jerusalem from all over the world. A large crowd heard the noise and excitement and came to see what was happening.

"Do you remember Jesus, who died?" Peter asked them. "He is alive! He is the new king you were waiting for. Now he has given us a gift—his Holy Spirit.

"If you ask God for his forgiveness, he will give you the very same gift!"

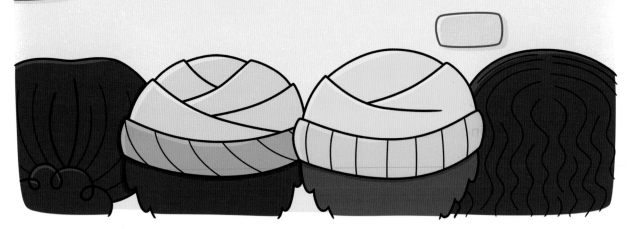

On that day hundreds of people decided that they too wanted to live life with God, to live the way he had made them to live.

These new followers of Jesus learned together, ate meals together, loved each other, and shared everything they had. When people needed help, they helped. When someone needed money, they sold their belongings and gave their money away.

And every day they thanked God for everything he had done for them.

This was the first church!

APOSTLE PAUL

Very soon people started to notice how the members of this new church looked after each other and took care of others. People wanted to be a part of it.

They were excited about God and excited about his church.

Well, not everyone was excited about it. There was a man called Saul who hated what was happening. He wanted to stop it before it could get any bigger, so he hunted for people who loved Jesus and put them in prison. Saul was an enemy to God.

But God had a plan for him.

One day Saul was traveling with some friends to a city called Damascus, in search of Jesus' followers.

But as he was walking along the road, a bright, blinding light flashed down from the sky. It was all around him, and it was so bright that Saul couldn't see a thing.

Then he heard a voice say, "Saul, why are you doing this to me?"

"Who are you?" said Saul.

"I am Jesus," said the voice. "Go into the city and you will be told what to do."

The light disappeared. Saul's friends were confused. They had heard the same voice but they hadn't seen anything.

Saul stood up and opened his eyes. He couldn't see.

He was blind!

His friends had to help him by holding his hands as they walked into Damascus.

In the same city, God had told a man called Ananias to go and find Saul. Ananias loved God but he did not like this idea at all. He knew that Saul hated God's people (and that meant him too).

But God told Ananias that he had a plan for this enemy. A surprising plan. He was going to change Saul's heart and use him to tell the story of God's love to people everywhere.

Saul was going to become someone who loved God instead of hating him. He was going to teach God's people instead of hurting them.

Because Ananias loved God, he did what he was asked.

Ananias put his hands on Saul and said, "Jesus has sent me to you so that you can see again, and have the gift of his Holy Spirit."

Suddenly Saul could see again! God had healed his eyes—and he had also changed Saul's heart.

Now Saul wanted to help God's church. Instead of arresting Jesus' followers, he wanted to be their friend.

The people in Damascus were amazed. "Is this the same man who used to hate God's people?" they asked.

It was. God had changed Saul.

And now he could tell others that Jesus was the new King, the Son of God.

Because Saul had changed so much, he wanted to change his name too. So he became Paul instead of Saul.

Paul traveled far and wide telling people about Jesus and helping them to follow God and live close to him.

Small groups of followers grew in many different places— new churches made up of people that loved God and wanted to follow him.

Paul wrote letters to all these churches, helping people understand how Jesus wanted them to live. He taught them how to love God, obey him, and love each other.

God had set apart a tribe to show the world who he was.

He had sent Jesus to show the world how much he loved them.

And now he was sending Paul out into the world to start telling that story to everyone, everywhere.

THE KINGDOM OF HEAVEN

At the beginning of everything, God made us to be his children. He made us to love him, to be loved by him, and to love each other. He gave us an incredible world in which everything had its place, and where our place was close to him.

That's what we were made for.

When Adam and Eve stopped trusting God, the world became broken. Things were no longer as they were meant to be. People kept forgetting God's love and stopped trusting him (just like we sometimes do).

But because God's love never changes, he had a plan to bring his children back to him—an amazing, costly plan. God sent Jesus to show us his love; to be everything we need.

All we have to do is trust him.

This is the best news in the world!

But even that isn't the end of the story!

God has promised that one day all the broken things in the world will be made right. There will be no more sadness, or sickness, or death.

One day the kingdom of heaven will come to earth, and EVERYTHING will be made new again.

Then we will be where we were made to be right from the start—living close to God, loving him, and being loved by him forever.

And nothing will ever change that.

IN THE MEANTIME...

This is the biggest and most important story in
the world. And because we are all God's children,
it's our story too. We all have a part to play.

God wants to fix the broken things in the world,
and we get to help.

Jesus shows us how. We need to ...

Love God with our whole heart.
Love everyone the way God loves us.
Love our enemies and do good to those who hurt us.

This is what we were made for!

And this is how we become part of the new creation,
where broken things are made right ...

Until God returns and makes everything new again.

"He will live with them, and they will be his people. God
himself will be with them. He will wipe every tear from
their eyes, and there will be no more death or sorrow or
crying or pain. All these things are gone forever [...]
'Look, I am making everything new!'"

–Revelation 21:3-5 (NLT)